I Wonde

QUESTIONS & ANSWERS ABOUT

ANIMALS

KINGFISHER

KINGFISHER
An imprint of Kingfisher Publications Plc
New Penderel House
283–288 High Holborn
London WC1V 7HZ

Material in this edition previously published by Kingfisher in the
I Wonder Why series

This edition first published by Kingfisher Publications Plc 1998

10 9 8 7 6 5 4 3 2 1

A CIP catalogue record for this book is available from the
British Library.

ISBN 0 7534 0276 9

Printed in Italy

I Wonder Why Series:
Editor: Clare Oliver, Brigid Avison, Jackie Gaff, Clare Llewellen
Design: David West Children's Books
Additional design: Smiljka Surla
Art editor: Christina Fraser

Questions & Answers About Animals:
Assistant editor: Christian Lewis
Cover design: Mike Smith

Contents

![] Endangered species

● Female Queen Alexandra's birdwings are the world's biggest butterflies. Their wings are almost as big as this page!

● The blue whale is so long that eight elephants could stand along its back.

Giraffe
5.5 metres tall

Elephant
3.5 metres tall
7 tonnes

Ostrich
2.5 metres tall

● The giraffe is the tallest land animal. With its long neck, it can reach as high as a two-storey house.

● The mighty African elephant is almost three times as tall as you are. It can weigh as much as seven cars.

● The ostrich is the world's tallest and heaviest bird. It's as tall as a single-decker bus!

Which is the biggest animal?

The biggest animal that has ever lived is the blue whale – it is even larger than the biggest dinosaurs were. Blue whales can weigh as much as 150 cars!

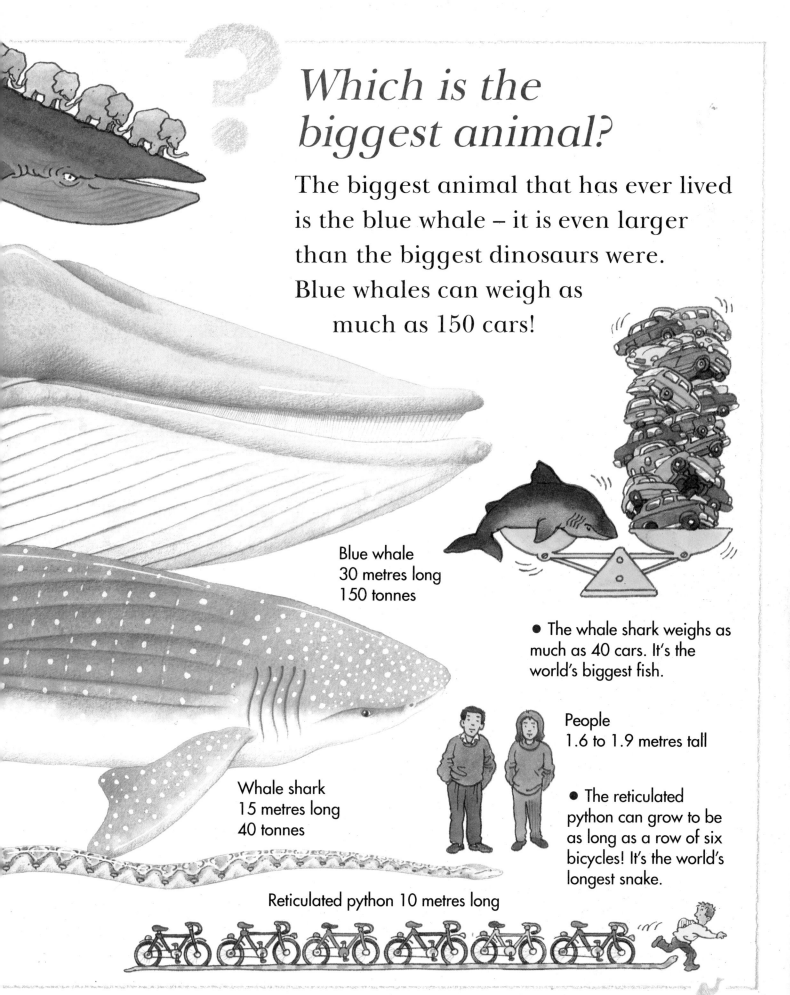

Blue whale
30 metres long
150 tonnes

● The whale shark weighs as much as 40 cars. It's the world's biggest fish.

People
1.6 to 1.9 metres tall

● The reticulated python can grow to be as long as a row of six bicycles! It's the world's longest snake.

Whale shark
15 metres long
40 tonnes

Reticulated python 10 metres long

What's the difference between frogs and toads?

Frogs usually have smooth skin and long legs for leaping. Most toads have lumpy skin and move their short thick bodies about by crawling.

Toad

Frog

...and alligators and crocodiles?

Crocodiles have longer, more pointed snouts than alligators. Crocodiles also have one very large tooth sticking up on each side when they close their mouths.

• Frogs and toads are both amphibians.

• Alligators and crocodiles are reptiles.

Crocodile

Alligator

...and between monkeys and apes?

The big difference between these animals is that monkeys have long tails, but apes don't have tails at all. There are lots of different kinds of monkey, but the only apes are gorillas, orang-utans, chimpanzees and gibbons.

Spider monkey

Orang-utan (ape)

● Monkeys and apes are mammals

● A woodlouse looks like it's an insect, but it isn't – it has too many legs! This creepy-crawly is related to crabs and lobsters.

● Rabbits and hares are both mammals.

...and rabbits and hares?

Hares have longer legs and ears than rabbits. Their whiskers are longer, too.

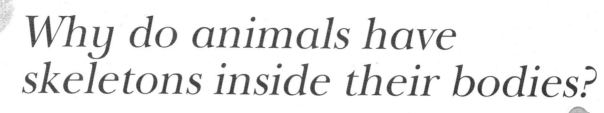

Why do animals have skeletons inside their bodies?

Not all animals have skeletons, but most large ones do. This is because the bigger an animal is, the more it needs a strong sturdy framework to hold its body together and carry its weight. Skeletons also protect soft inside parts, like brains and hearts.

Backbone

● Animals without backbones are called invertebrates. Insects, spiders, snails, worms, jellyfish, prawns and crabs are all invertebrates.

● Animals with backbones are called vertebrates. Fish are vertebrates, and so are amphibians, reptiles, birds and mammals.

Backbone

- Most animals' skeletons are made of bone, but a shark's skeleton is made of gristle. This isn't as hard as bone, but it's still tough. You have some at your nose tip.

Millipede

- Insects, spiders, scorpions, centipedes and millipedes all have tough exoskeletons.

- Lobsters, crabs and some beetles have really tough exoskeletons that work like armour, to protect them from attack.

- Squid are the biggest kind of invertebrate. The longest one ever found measured more than 17 metres from its head to the tip of its tentacles – longer than eight scuba divers!

Which animals have skeletons on the outside?

Most smaller animals have tough skins called exoskeletons. These outside skeletons do the same job as inside ones. They protect and support the animals' soft bodies.

- To grow larger, an animal has to break out of its old exoskeleton and grow a new one.

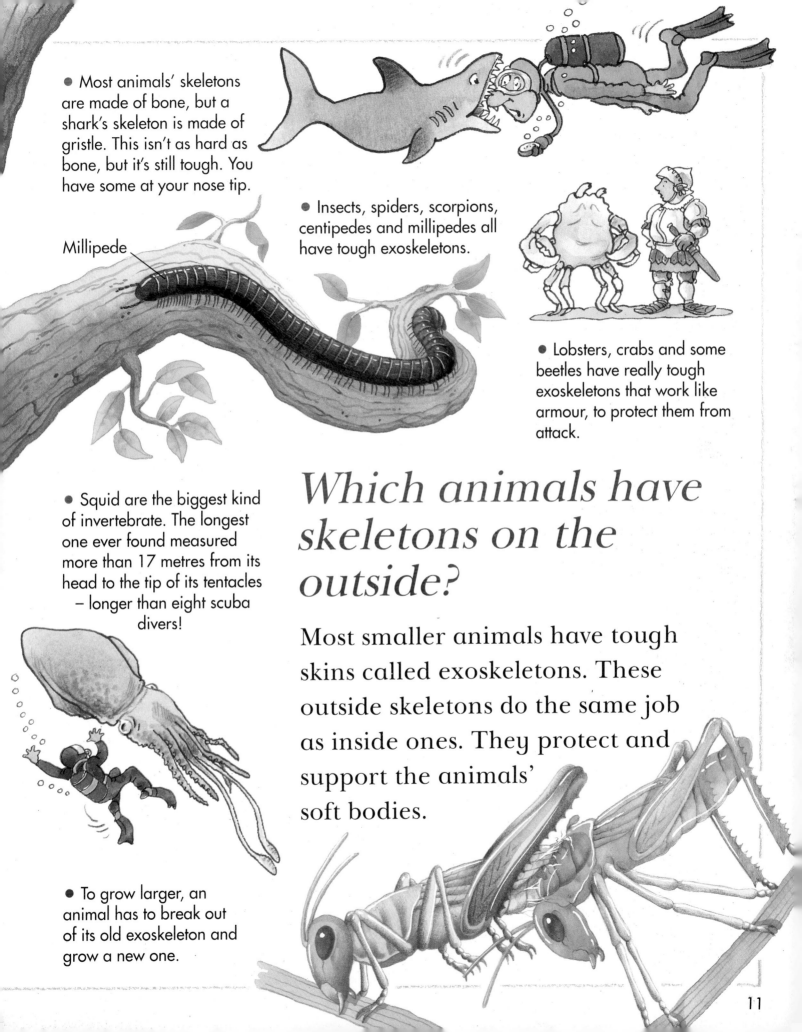

Why are zebras stripy?

No one knows for sure why zebras have stripy coats, but it must help them to see each other so that they can stay together in a herd. There's safety in numbers, of course – especially against hungry lions!

● No two zebras have exactly the same pattern of stripes – just as no two people have exactly the same fingerprints!

● Some things give you spots in front of your eyes, but a herd of galloping zebras would give you stripes! For a lion, it must be even harder to pick which zebra to chase.

Why do leopards have spots?

A leopard's spots help it to hide among trees and bushes, so it can pounce out and surprise its prey. The light and dark patches in its fur match the patches of sunlight and shadow under the leafy branches.

Which animal changes colour?

Chameleons usually have browny green skin, but it only takes them a few minutes to change their colour completely!

These strange animals can change colour to match things around them, which helps them hide from enemies. Chameleons also change colour when angry or frightened.

● The fur of some animals that live in cold countries is brown in summer and white in winter. This makes it harder to see the animals when snow covers the ground.

Why are flamingoes pink?

Flamingoes take their pink colour from their favourite food – shrimps! If these leggy birds don't get enough shrimps to eat, they turn a dull grey.

Which bird has eyes in the back of its head?

An owl's eyes aren't really in the back of its head, but at times they might as well be! Owls have such bendy necks that when they want to look backwards they swivel their heads right around!

● An owl's huge eyes help it to see at night. This is when most owls fly about hunting for food.

How do bats see in the dark?

Bats not only speed about at night without bumping into things, they also manage to hunt down juicy insects to eat. Bats can do this even when it's pitch dark, because they use sound not light to find their way.

● Bats make lots of very high squeaking sounds as they fly about. When these sounds hit objects – like insects or trees – they bounce off them, back towards the bats. The repeated sounds are called echoes. And bats can tell where things are by listening to them.

● The blue-tongued skink sticks out its big blue tongue to frighten enemies away.

● Starfish don't have heads, but they do have eyes. They are on the ends of their arms.

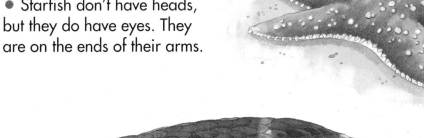

Which animals smell with their tongues?

Snakes and lizards don't smell with their noses like we do. Instead, they flick their long tongues in and out. Their tongues pick up smells from the air and the ground, helping them to track down things to eat.

● African elephants have ears as big as bedspreads – the biggest ears in the world. Elephants have very good hearing, but their ears are also useful for keeping cool. They can be flapped like fans, for example.

Why do camels have humps?

A camel's hump is its own built-in food cupboard. By living off the fat stored in its hump, a camel can go for as long as two weeks without eating. Camels need their humps because they live in deserts, where food and water are hard to find.

Why do elephants have trunks?

An elephant's trunk is a helpful tool. It can be used to pull down leaves and branches to eat. It also makes a good hose – elephants can squirt dust or water over themselves to keep cool.

● Elephants say 'hello' to friends by shaking trunks with them.

● An elephant's trunk is a bit like a hand. Using its tip, an elephant can pick up something as small as a button.

● Arabian camels have one hump.

Land animals

Why do giraffes have long necks?

A giraffe's long neck makes it tall enough to eat the leaves at the top of trees. Other animals cannot reach as high, so the giraffe has lots to eat.

● A giraffe's tongue is half a metre long!

How high can a kangaroo hop?

Believe it or not, big kangaroos can hop right over your head! As far as we know, the highest a kangaroo has ever jumped is roughly 3 metres – more than twice as high as you are. Their big strong back legs help kangaroos to be such good high-jumpers.

● For their size, fleas are the world's best high-jumpers. They can jump over 100 times their own height.

● By hopping in giant leaps, big kangaroos can move nearly as fast as racehorses!

How fast can a cheetah run?

● Cheetahs use their sharp claws to grip and push against the ground as they race along. Olympic runners have spikes on their shoes for the same reason.

A hungry cheetah can sprint faster than 100 kilometres per hour when chasing something to eat. But running this fast soon wears it out, and it has to stop to get its breath back.

● Kangaroos use their tails to balance as they hop. They'd probably fall flat on their faces if they didn't.

Which animal has an extra hand?

Some South American monkeys can grip tree branches with just their tails, leaving their hands free to pick fruit and nuts to eat. Unlike most monkeys, whose tails are completely covered with fur, they have bare skin at the end of their tails – rather like the palm of your hand.

● Sloths are very strange slow South American animals. They creep upside down through the treetops, and it can take them a day to move 100 metres!

Why do orang-utans need all the trees?

Orang-utans are rainforest animals that spend all their lives in the trees. When trees are cut down, gaps are left in the forest, and the orang-utans can't move about looking for food or places to sleep.

• There are more kinds of tree and animal in the rainforests than in any other place. When the trees are cut down, all the living things in the forests are in danger.

Which endangered animal is the shyest?

The shy okapi is so hard to find that scientists didn't even know it existed until 1901! Today there are fewer okapis than ever, because their rainforest home is being cut down.

Why is it bad luck to be an aye-aye?

Aye-ayes feed at night in the rain-forests of Madagascar. Some of the people of that island think that aye-ayes bring bad luck, so they kill them. The animals are extremely rare, but in some places they are now protected.

● Rainforest hunters have used poison from arrow-poison frogs on the tips of their arrows for centuries. But now the frogs may become endangered because so many are being collected to sell as pets.

Which fox flies to its food?

The Rodrigues flying fox isn't a fox at all. It's a bat that lives on Rodrigues Island in the Indian Ocean. It eats fruit, so it needs lots of fruit trees. Sadly, most of its forest home has been cut down and there are now only 400 bats left.

How many ants can an anteater eat?

On a good day, a giant anteater eats an amazing 30,000 ants! It can scoop up as many as 500 with each flick of its long sticky tongue. Anteaters don't munch their food because they haven't any teeth. They swallow the ants whole.

• Giant anteaters have to walk on the knuckles of their front feet because their claws are so long and sharp. They use these claws to rip ant hills apart.

• Birds that feed on fish often have long sharp beaks. The anhinga uses its beak to spear fish.

• Bears tear bees' nests apart to get at the honey inside. They don't seem to mind getting stung.

Which animal uses its finger as a fork?

A strange monkey-like animal called an aye-aye has one very long thin finger on each hand. It uses these spindly fingers to poke under tree bark for grubs and insects to eat. Then it skewers them, using its fingers a bit like you would use a fork.

● Aye-ayes only live on the island of Madagascar, off the east coast of Africa.

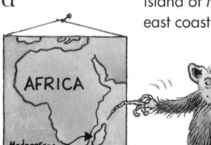

Which is the greediest animal?

For its size, the tiny Etruscan shrew has the world's biggest appetite. It hardly ever stops eating! By the time it's full grown, it has to eat three times its own weight in food each day.

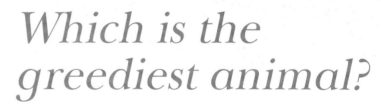

● An adult Etruscan shrew weighs less than a sugar lump.

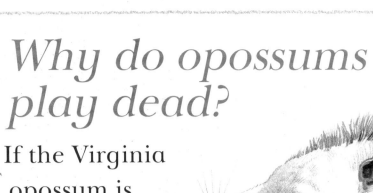

Why do opossums play dead?

If the Virginia opossum is attacked, it sometimes tries to fool its enemy into leaving it alone by playing dead. Its eyes go glassy, and it lies quite still with its tongue hanging out. It's more usual – and safer – for an opossum to run away, though, or to climb a tree!

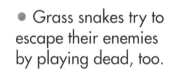

● Grass snakes try to escape their enemies by playing dead, too.

Which is the smelliest animal?

The skunk is a very smelly creature. If an enemy makes the mistake of getting too close, the skunk sprays it with a stinking oily liquid. The terrible smell can last for days!

Which is the prickliest animal?

Porcupines are pricklier than any pincushion. Their backs are covered in hundreds of long sharp quills, with barbs like fishhooks on the ends.

- If a porcupine is attacked, it raises and spreads its quills, rattling them as a warning. Then it rushes backwards towards its enemy.

- Some crabs have their own bodyguards. They carry a sea anemone in each claw so that the anemones' tentacles can sting any enemies that get too close.

- Porcupine fish blow themselves up into prickly balls when enemies attack.

How do fish breathe under water?

▷ Not all sea creatures can breathe under water. Sea cows, seals and dolphins breathe air, so they have to keep coming to the surface.

Fish have to breathe to stay alive, just as you do. But while you breathe oxygen from the air, fish take it from water. As they swim, fish gulp in water and push it out through slits called gills on their heads.

Oxygen passes from the water into the fish's blood inside their gills.

Gill cover

How do fish swim?

Fish swim by using their muscles to ripple their bodies along. Wiggling their tails from side to side gives them extra push. They use their other fins to balance and change direction.

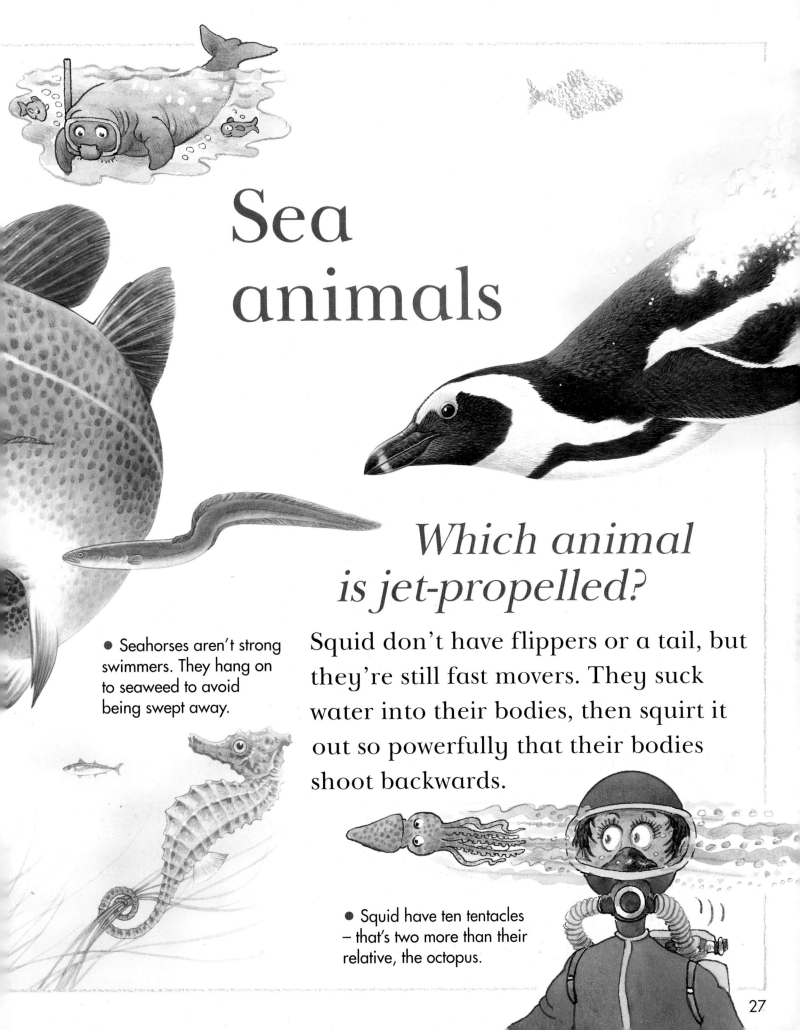

Sea animals

Which animal is jet-propelled?

Squid don't have flippers or a tail, but they're still fast movers. They suck water into their bodies, then squirt it out so powerfully that their bodies shoot backwards.

● Seahorses aren't strong swimmers. They hang on to seaweed to avoid being swept away.

● Squid have ten tentacles – that's two more than their relative, the octopus.

Which is the biggest fish?

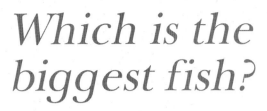

The whale shark is the world's biggest fish. It's gigantic – as long as eight scuba divers lying head to toe, and as heavy as six large elephants.

● The dwarf goby is the smallest fish in the ocean.

● The oar fish is the longest fish in the ocean – as long as four canoes placed end to end.

Oar fish

● The biggest sea plant is the giant kelp seaweed. A single strand can grow nearly as long as a football pitch!

Sailfish

Which is the fastest fish?

The sailfish can race along under water at over 100 kilometres an hour – as fast as a car. It tucks its fins in tightly, and its pointed nose cuts through the water like a knife.

Whale shark

Which is the biggest crab?

● The pea-sized pea crab is the smallest crab of all. It lives inside oyster and mussel shells.

Japan's giant spider crab measures nearly 4 metres from the tip of one front claw to the tip of the other. It could open its arms wide enough to hug a hippopotamus!

Which fish hunts with a hammer?

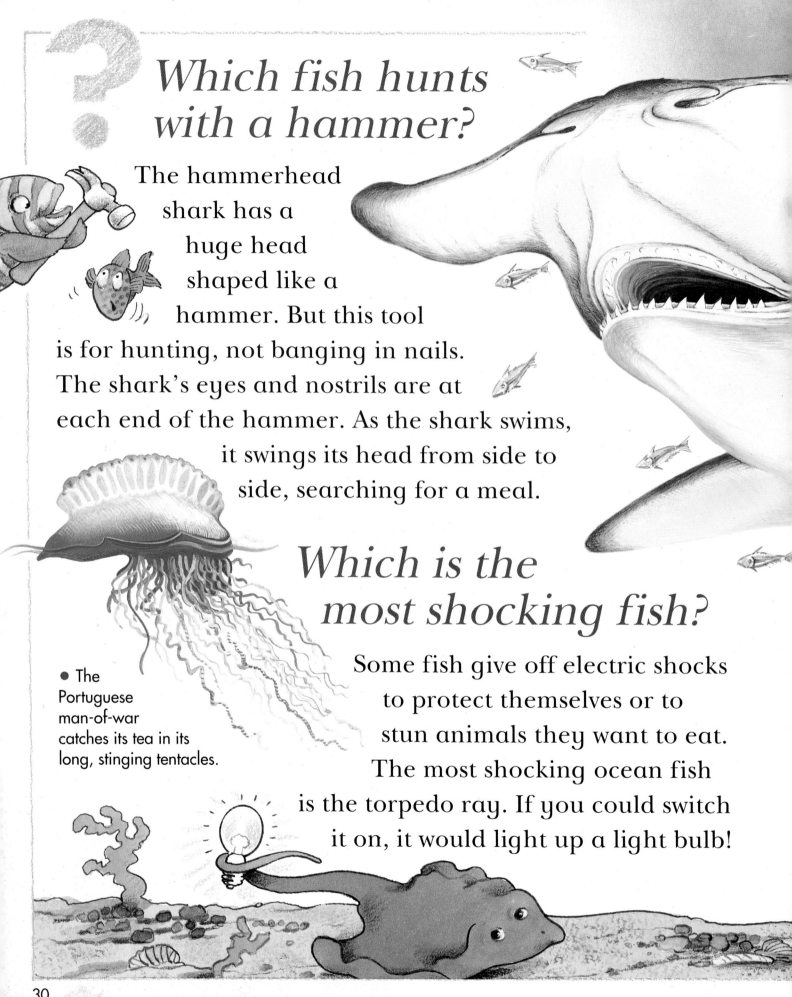

The hammerhead shark has a huge head shaped like a hammer. But this tool is for hunting, not banging in nails. The shark's eyes and nostrils are at each end of the hammer. As the shark swims, it swings its head from side to side, searching for a meal.

● The Portuguese man-of-war catches its tea in its long, stinging tentacles.

Which is the most shocking fish?

Some fish give off electric shocks to protect themselves or to stun animals they want to eat. The most shocking ocean fish is the torpedo ray. If you could switch it on, it would light up a light bulb!

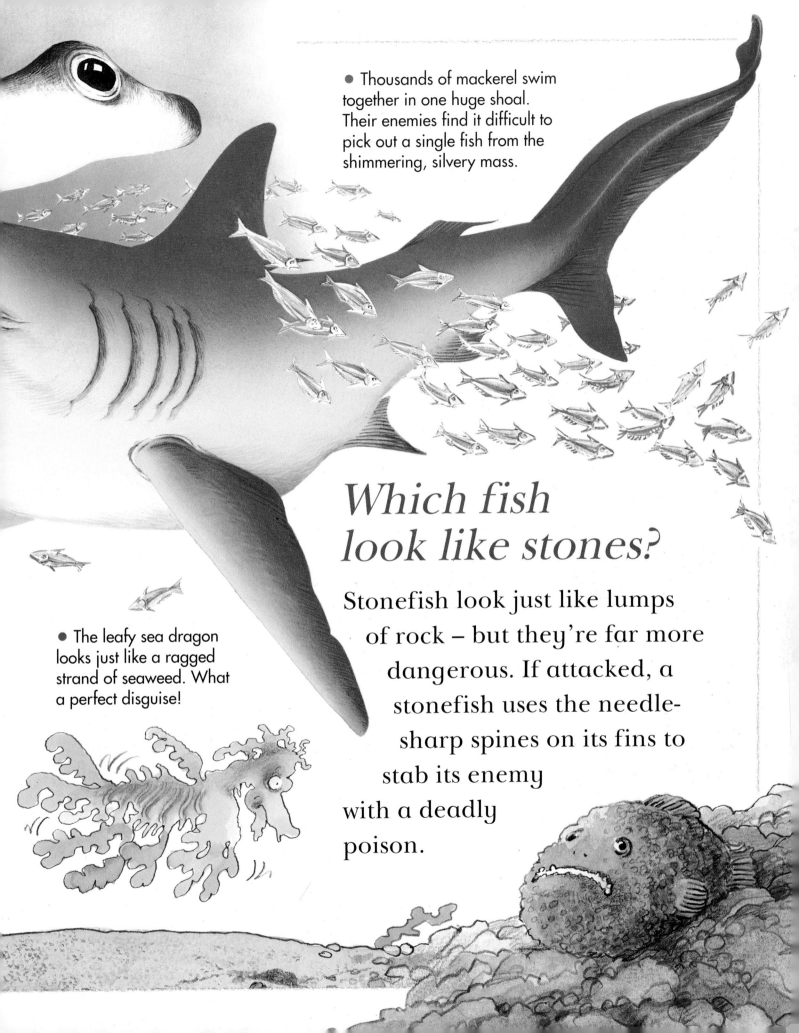

● Thousands of mackerel swim together in one huge shoal. Their enemies find it difficult to pick out a single fish from the shimmering, silvery mass.

Which fish look like stones?

Stonefish look just like lumps of rock – but they're far more dangerous. If attacked, a stonefish uses the needle-sharp spines on its fins to stab its enemy with a deadly poison.

● The leafy sea dragon looks just like a ragged strand of seaweed. What a perfect disguise!

Where do angels, clowns and parrots live?

Angelfish, clownfish and parrotfish are just some of the thousands of beautiful animals that live on coral reefs. Tropical fish like these often have dazzling colours and bold patterns.

Imperial angelfish

Parrotfish

● Coral reefs grow in shallow water in the warmest parts of the world.

Angelfish

● Giant clams live on coral reefs. Their shells are big enough to have a bath in!

32

What is a coral reef?

A coral reef is like a beautiful underwater hedge. It looks stony and dead – but it is really alive! Coral is made up of millions of tiny animals, which leave their hard skeletons behind when they die. Each new layer piles on to the old, slowly building the coral rock.

● Corals comes in all sorts of shapes – antlers, plates, mushrooms, feathers, daisies and even brains!

Where is the biggest reef?

The world's biggest coral reef lies in warm shallow seas off the northeast coast of Australia. It's called the Great Barrier Reef, and it stretches for more than 2,000 kilometres. It's so huge that it can be seen by astronauts up in space.

Clown fish

Why do birds fly?

Flying is a great way to escape from enemies. With a few flaps of its wings, a bird can get to a safe perch well out of the reach of a hungry cat! Being able to fly also helps birds to move quickly from one feeding ground to another, and to catch insects that buzz through the air.

● The handsome roller bird is a true acrobat. When chasing insects, it performs somersaults in the air.

Birds

How do birds fly?

The usual way for a bird to fly is to flap its wings up and down. This pushes it through the air, just as oars push a boat through the water. But it's hard work, so some birds save energy by gliding. Once they've built up speed, they spread out their wings, and let breezy air currents carry them along.

● Like planes, birds need to be strong but light. To keep their weight down, they have hollow or paper-thin bones.

● Hummingbirds are the only birds that can fly backwards. They can also fly forwards, sideways and upside-down!

● The common swift spends nearly its whole life in the air. It even sleeps on the wing!

Which bird is a giant?

The ostrich is the biggest living bird. From top to toe it's over 2.5 metres tall – that's about as high as the ceiling! And it's heavy, too, weighing about the same as a Shetland pony!

• The biggest flying bird is the wandering albatross. From wingtip to wingtip it's as long as a family car!

• The ostrich can't fly. But it can run from danger at up to 72 kilometres per hour – that's faster than a racehorse.

Ostrich

Which bird flies fastest?

Eider duck

The eider duck can fly along at up to 100 kilometres per hour. But the real record-breaker is the peregrine falcon. It swoops down on its prey at over 200 kilometres per hour, making it the fastest animal on Earth.

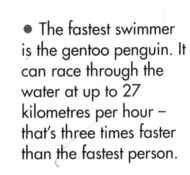

Peregrine falcon

● The fastest swimmer is the gentoo penguin. It can race through the water at up to 27 kilometres per hour – that's three times faster than the fastest person.

Which is the smallest bird?

● The African kori bustard is the heaviest flying bird. Sometimes it even has trouble getting off the ground!

In tropical rainforests, many of the birds are smaller than the butterflies. The Cuban bee hummingbird is probably the smallest of all. It's about as big as the eye of an ostrich – and can perch on the end of a pencil.

37

Why are birds special?

Birds are not the only animals with wings, the only ones that lay eggs, or the only ones with beaks. But they are the only creatures in the whole wide world that have feathers.

● Birds aren't the only animals to fly. Bats do, too – and they're mammals.

● Birds aren't the only animals to have a beak. The duck-billed platypus does, too.

● Birds aren't the only animals to lay eggs. Tortoises and other reptiles do, too.

● All birds have wings, but not all of them can fly. Some creep, hop, or run along the ground; others swim like seals in the sea.

● There are 30 birds in the world for every man, woman and child.

Which birds have scales?

All of them! Birds' feet and legs are covered with scaly skin, just like the skin of snakes and lizards. That's why you never see birds wearing shoes and socks! But the scales don't stop there. A bird's feathers may seem soft to the touch, but they're made of tough, horny stuff – just like scales.

39

How many feathers does a bird have?

The bigger a bird is, the more feathers it has. A hummingbird has about 900 feathers, while a swan has 25,000! Feathers come in all different shapes and sizes. Soft downy feathers keep the bird warm, others keep it waterproof in the rain, and the strongest feathers give it the power to fly.

● Birds have long tail feathers, smooth wing and body feathers, and fluffy down feathers. Down is warmer than fur – it's like a bird's woolly underwear.

Tail feathers

Golden pheasant

Pheasant

Down feather

Body feathers

Parrot

African grey parrot

Goose

Scarlet macaw

Guinea fowl

● Every wing feather is made up of hundreds of hair-like strands. These zip together with tiny hooks to make a smooth, strong blade.

Why are vultures bald?

Vultures are messy eaters. They feed on dead animals, pushing their heads right inside the bodies to tear into the meat. If they had head feathers, they'd get dirty and sticky, and would be almost impossible to clean. That's why vultures are much better off being bald.

● Feathers work so hard that they wear out. The bird grows a new set each year and the old ones gradually fall out. This is called moulting.

Wing feathers

Parrot

Seagull

Macaw

Flamingo

Turkey

● Before pens were invented, people wrote with quills. These were large feathers, sharpened at the end and dipped in ink.

Which animals are reptiles?

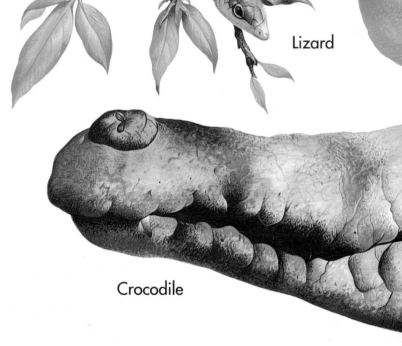

Snakes, lizards, crocodiles and turtles all belong to the same animal group – the reptiles. All reptiles have a bony skeleton and a scaly skin. Most of them lay eggs, which hatch on land. But some reptiles give birth to their babies.

Lizard

Crocodile

● Reptiles live on land and in the sea almost everywhere on Earth. But they don't like the cold, so you won't find them around the Poles.

Are frogs and newts reptiles?

Frogs and newts are not reptiles. They have no scales, and their skin is very thin. They lay their eggs in water, and their young hatch out as tadpoles. Baby reptiles look just like their parents, only smaller.

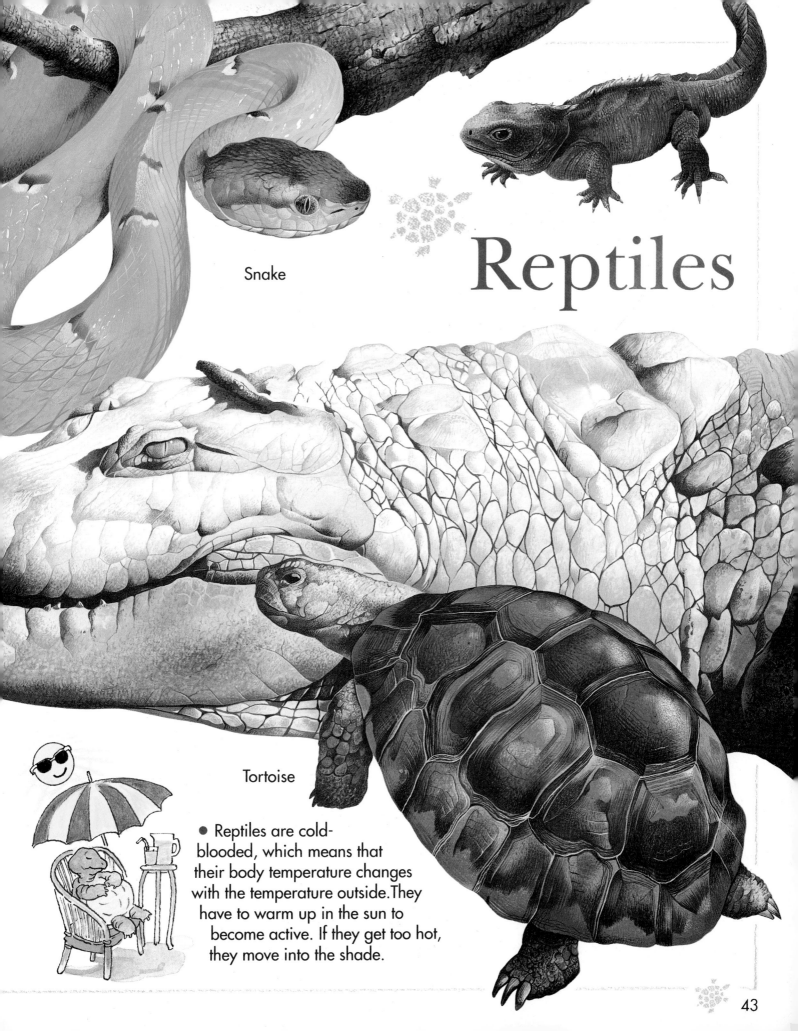

Snake

Reptiles

Tortoise

● Reptiles are cold-
blooded, which means that
their body temperature changes
with the temperature outside. They
have to warm up in the sun to
become active. If they get too hot,
they move into the shade.

43

Which is the biggest reptile?

The world's biggest reptile is the saltwater crocodile of tropical Asia and Australia. This huge beast can grow to over 7 metres – as wide as a football goal.

• The fastest reptile is a North American lizard called the six-lined racerunner. It could easily outrun you in a race – over short distances, it reaches speeds of 29 kilometres an hour!

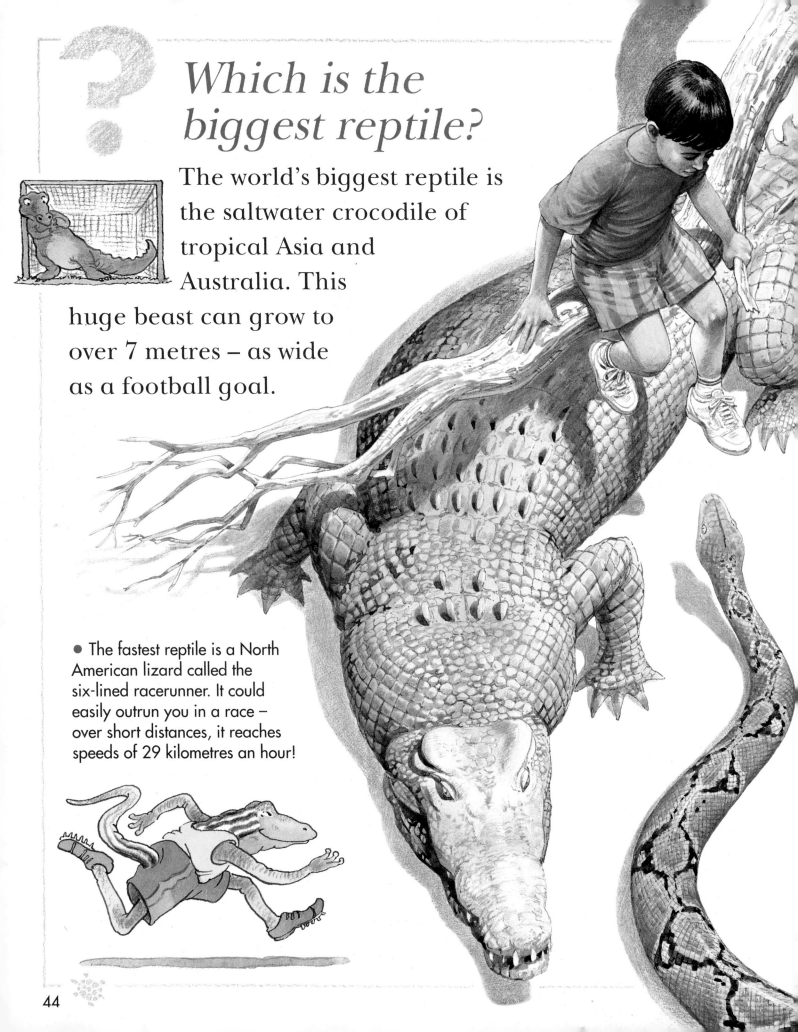

● The most spectacular reptiles have been dead for over 65 million years. They were the dinosaurs, the prehistoric relatives of today's reptiles.

Which reptile lives the longest?

Tortoises can live to a ripe old age. The oldest one ever known lived to be 152 years old! But this might not be a record – there could be even older tortoises in the wild.

● The smallest reptile is a tiny gecko lizard from the West Indies. It measures 3.5 centimetres from nose to tail, and would fit inside a book of matches with room to spare.

Which is the biggest snake?

The biggest snake is the anaconda of South America, which grows up to 10 metres – that's as long as a bus. The reticulated python is another whopper, but although it's as long as the anaconda, it's not as heavy

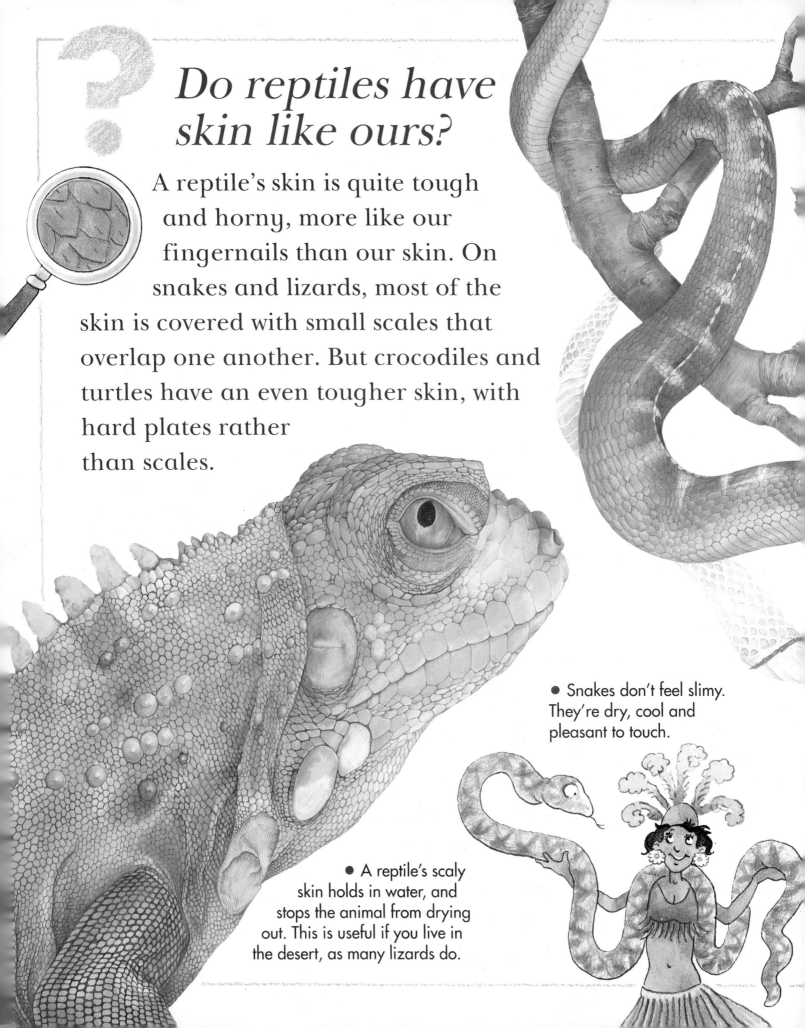

Do reptiles have skin like ours?

A reptile's skin is quite tough and horny, more like our fingernails than our skin. On snakes and lizards, most of the skin is covered with small scales that overlap one another. But crocodiles and turtles have an even tougher skin, with hard plates rather than scales.

● Snakes don't feel slimy. They're dry, cool and pleasant to touch.

● A reptile's scaly skin holds in water, and stops the animal from drying out. This is useful if you live in the desert, as many lizards do.

• A snake's old skin begins to split at the lips. The snake wriggles out head first, turning the skin inside out as it goes. The skin often comes off in one piece, in a perfect snake shape.

Why do snakes shed their skin?

Like your old clothes, a snake's skin wears out and needs replacing – often in a bigger size. So from three to seven times a year, the old skin splits open and peels off, and – hey presto! – there's a brand-new skin waiting underneath.

• In times of danger, the armadillo lizard turns into an armoured ball. It rolls on its back, grips its tail in its mouth and hides its soft belly behind a wall of scales and spines.

Why do some lizards have horns and spikes?

Horns and spikes are a good way of protecting an animal. Like a strong suit of armour, they make a lizard look fierce – and they also make a prickly mouthful for any animal that tries to attack.

Whose tongue is longer than its tail?

The chameleon's sticky-tipped tongue isn't just longer than its tail, it's longer than its whole body! The lizard shoots it out in a twinkling and reels it back in with a meal.

Why do lizards lose their tails?

Lizards can snap off their tails when they're being attacked. The dropped tail wriggles, puzzling the enemy, and giving the lizard time to escape. A new tail grows in a few weeks.

Why do geckos lick their eyes?

Most lizards have eyelids to wipe their eyes, but the gecko doesn't. Like a snake, it has a scale across the eye. To keep its eyes moist and squeaky clean, the gecko licks them, using its long tongue like a handy wipe.

● Most lizards are land-lubbers. The marine iguana from the Galápagos Islands is the only one that lives in the sea.

Are there still dragons on Earth?

The Komodo dragon may not have wings or breathe fire, but it is truly awesome. It's the world's largest lizard – longer than a car, and heavier than a couple of prize-fighters. When people first saw one about 100 years ago, they thought they were looking at a dragon!

What is an insect?

An insect has three pairs of legs (that's six altogether), and three parts to its body. The first part is the head, the second is the thorax, and the third is the abdomen.

- Like all insects, this hoverfly has three pairs of legs and three parts to its body.

Feeler
Head
Eye
Thorax
Mouth
Leg

- Woodlice aren't insects. They belong to the same family as crabs, lobsters and shrimps. They don't get together very often though, as woodlice live on land, not in water.

When is a fly not a fly?

A true fly, such as a housefly, has only one pair of wings. Butterflies, dragonflies, damselflies, and mayflies all have two pairs of wings. So they're not really flies at all!

Wing

- Bedbugs are the draculas of the insect world. At night, they look for sleeping humans to bite. Then they suck up the tasty blood!

Insects

- Centipedes have too many legs to be insects. One kind has 176 pairs!

Abdomen

- There are over a million kinds of insect – more than any other kind of animal in the world. And scientists are still finding new ones!

Are spiders insects?

No – a spider has eight legs, not six. What's more, its body has two parts instead of three. This is because the head and thorax are joined on a spider's body.

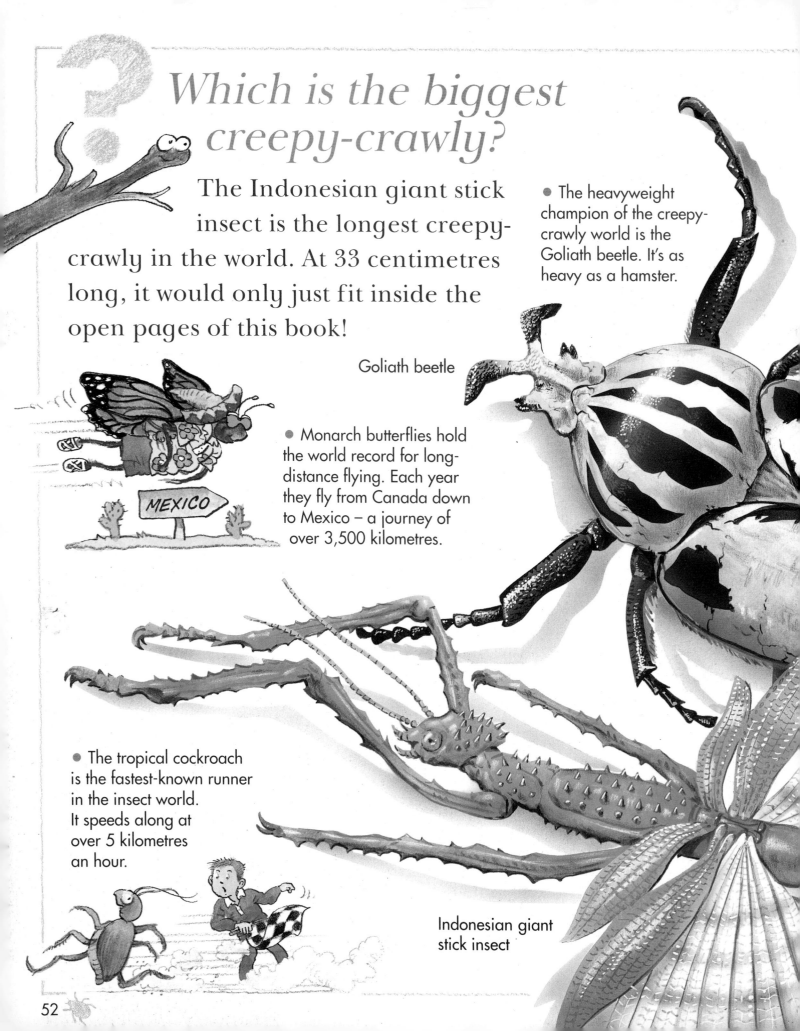

Which is the biggest creepy-crawly?

The Indonesian giant stick insect is the longest creepy-crawly in the world. At 33 centimetres long, it would only just fit inside the open pages of this book!

Goliath beetle

● The heavyweight champion of the creepy-crawly world is the Goliath beetle. It's as heavy as a hamster.

MEXICO

● Monarch butterflies hold the world record for long-distance flying. Each year they fly from Canada down to Mexico – a journey of over 3,500 kilometres.

● The tropical cockroach is the fastest-known runner in the insect world. It speeds along at over 5 kilometres an hour.

Indonesian giant stick insect

Which is the smallest creepy-crawly?

● Before the time of the dinosaurs, monster-sized dragonflies cruised through the air. Some were the size of seagulls!

You'd find it hard to see a fairy fly, because it's no bigger than a full stop. The female lays her tiny eggs inside the eggs of other insects. She can squeeze as many as 20 into just one butterfly egg.

● The Hercules emperor moth is the world's widest creepy-crawly. From wing to wing, it's the size of a dinner plate!

Why do caterpillars change into butterflies?

Every butterfly has to go through four different stages of its life before it is a fully grown adult. At each stage, it changes its size, its shape and its colour.

● Many kinds of insect change shape as they grow. This way of growing is called metamorphosis.

1 A butterfly lays its eggs on a plant the baby caterpillars eat.

2 The caterpillars eat hungrily, and grow very quickly.

● The babies that hatch from an insect's eggs are known as larvae – but many people just call them grubs.

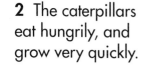

● Caterpillars grow so quickly that their skin pops open. Underneath, there's brand new skin with plenty of growing room.

3 Each caterpillar makes itself a hard case called a pupa. Inside, its body turns into a kind of mushy soup.

● The pupa is like a strongbox. It keeps the insect's body safe while it changes shape.

NO ENTRY
REBUILDING
WORK
IN PROGRESS

- Nymphs split their skins as they grow, but they don't make a pupa. They just slowly change into adults.

- Not all insects change completely as they grow. A grasshopper's eggs hatch out into tiny nymphs, which look almost like their parents.

- A female butterfly lays as many as 50,000 eggs in her lifetime.

4 The soup slowly turns into a butterfly. When the butterfly wriggles out of the pupa, its wings are soft and creased. They dry in the sunlight.

- Butterflies don't need food to grow, but they love to sip sweet nectar from a flower now and then. It's a fuel that helps them to fly.

55

Which insects wear armour?

Beetles have two pairs of wings, but they only use one pair to fly. The other pair is like a thick piece of armour, covering the beetle's delicate wings and soft body.

1 When a beetle is scuttling along the ground, its flying wings are hidden beneath a shiny armoured wing casing.

2 When it wants to fly, a beetle opens its armour casing and stretches out its wings.

△ It's not difficult to guess how the giraffe weevil got its name. Its neck is twice as long as its body!

Which beetle fires a spray gun?

Watch out for the bombardier beetle! It shoots its enemies with a jet of hot, stinging liquid. As the jet is fired, it makes a sharp cracking sound like a tiny gun going off.

What digs graves, then robs them?

Burying beetles have no respect for the dead! When they find a dead animal, they dig away the soil until the body sinks into the ground. Then they lay their eggs inside the body and cover it with soil. When the eggs hatch out, there's a tasty, well-stocked meat store waiting for them!

- Imagine rolling balls of snow to make a snowman. That's how scarab beetles roll their balls of animal dung. They push the balls into a safe hiding place, and eat them later on.

- Ancient Egyptians thought the Sun was rolled across the sky by a giant scarab beetle.

3 The beetle beats its wings and moves smoothly through the air.

Which baby has the best mother?

A baby gorilla has one of the best mums in the world. A grown-up gorilla may look a bit frightening to us, but she's loving and gentle to her young. As well as grooming the baby, she feeds it for up to three years, and protects and helps it for longer still.

• Gorillas are a type of ape – along with chimpanzees, gibbons and orang-utans. All the apes make jolly good mums.

Baby animals

● The cuckoo manages to trick birds because her egg matches the other ones in the nest.

Which mother has her babies in prison?

While the female hornbill is laying her eggs in a hole in a tree, the male helps her to block up the door. But he leaves a hole for her beak so that he can feed her while she's stuck inside!

● Tree shrews are part-time mums. They leave their babies in the nest, only popping by to feed them every other day.

Which is the biggest baby in the world?

The baby blue whale is a real whopper, weighing up to 3,000 kilograms – that's as much as 1,000 human babies! As soon as it is born, its mum nudges it to the surface to take a first breath of air.

• A baby blue whale is as long as five scuba divers swimming tip to toe.

• The baby howler monkey is a champion screamer. Its cries can be heard even through thick rainforest.

Which is the tallest baby?

A baby giraffe is about two metres tall – that's taller than most grown-up people. The mother giraffe is taller still, and gives birth standing up. Her new baby hits the ground feet first. Ouch! It's a long way to fall.

● The young dragonfly must be one of the fiercest babies. It lives in rivers and lakes and grabs almost anything that moves with its spiky jaws.

Which is the ugliest baby?

One of the ugliest-looking babies is the vulture chick, with its big hooked beak and bare head and neck. But then its parents aren't very beautiful either. Maybe it comes from eating all that rotting meat!

Which baby has lots of aunties?

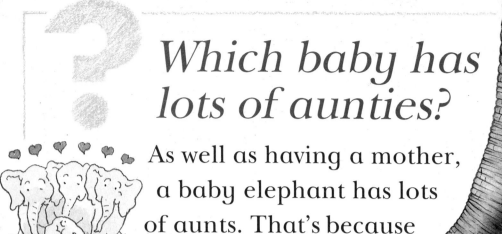

As well as having a mother, a baby elephant has lots of aunts. That's because female elephants live in large family groups of up to 50 animals. In fact, a new calf not only has plenty of aunts, it has grannies, sisters and cousins, too!

• When a hippo mother goes off to feed, she leaves her calf with a baby-sitter!

• Maras live in South America. They're a kind of long-legged guinea pig. Mara parents never join their babies in the burrow. They whistle down the hole and the young come scampering out.

Which babies stay in a nursery?

Mara parents leave their babies under ground. To make sure they aren't lonely, lots of families share the same burrow. When a mother drops by to feed her young, she checks up on the other mara babies, too.

- Bees use nurseries, too. The eggs hatch out in a special part of the hive.

Which is the biggest nursery?

- A bat mother has such sharp hearing that she recognises her baby's call from millions of others in the cave.

Bracken Cave in the United States is home to over twenty million bats. The mothers leave their babies in a nursery, huddled together for warmth. The bats are so tightly packed, there may be a thousand in a space the size of a doormat.

Why do lion cubs chase their mother's tail?

Lion cubs are very playful, and pounce on anything that moves – especially the tassel on the end of their mum's tail. Games like this teach the cubs how to chase and pounce – skills they'll need when they have to hunt for themselves.

● Sea otters know how to have fun. The mother tosses her baby into the air, and then catches it again. Wheeee!

● Play is how baby animals learn all sorts of important skills for grown-up life.

Why do ducklings play follow-my-leader?

When ducklings hatch, they follow the first moving thing they see, which is usually their mother. By following her everywhere, they learn how to swim and feed. And if they wander off, she only has to call and they fall in line!

● Some parents teach their young how to use tools. Baby chimps soon learn how to dig for termites with a stick.

● Bear cubs learn from their mother how to catch fish. They scoop them out of the river with their paws.

Which baby hides in the forest?

A young deer, called a fawn, is very wobbly on its legs. It couldn't outrun a hungry cougar or wolf! So when it senses danger, the young animal freezes and stays completely still until the danger has passed. The fawn's speckled coat helps it seem almost invisible in the forest's dappled light.

Which babies hide in a circle of horns?

Adult musk oxen make a circle around their calves when danger threatens. They stand close together, with their heads lowered, facing the enemy like a row of shields. It takes a brave and hungry wolf to attack the wall of long, curved horns!

• Lots of animals make noises to scare away enemies. Young burrowing owls, which live in holes in the ground, can make a noise like a rattlesnake when they are threatened.

Which mother pretends she's sick?

If a hungry hunter threatens a plover's nest, the mother bird pretends to be wounded. She flaps a wing as if it is broken and flutters weakly along the ground, moving away from the nest. She wants the enemy to think that she is injured and would be easy to capture. That way, the animal will go after her, not her babies.

• A mother scorpion protects her young for the first few days of their lives by carrying them on her back. If an enemy approaches, she arches her poison-tipped tail high above her back. That'll usually stop the enemy coming any closer!

Why are there no dinosaurs on Earth?

• Animals can become extinct because of things that people do. Or because the places they live in change.

The dinosaurs lived on Earth for millions of years. Then 65 million years ago, they became extinct – every single one of them disappeared. No one knows exactly what happened. One idea is that the world became too cold for them. Whatever the reason, there is none alive today.

Do all animals die out?

Every kind of animal dies out eventually. But new kinds of animal usually appear to take their place. These new species are often descendants of the extinct ones. For example, the elephants on Earth today are related to the hairy mammoths that disappeared about 10,000 years ago.

Endangered animals

● When people move to new parts of the world they often take animals with them. These new animals sometimes hunt the ones that already live there.

● Some animals are endangered because the places in which they live are cleared to make room for farms, factories, roads or houses.

Which endangered animal has a magic horn?

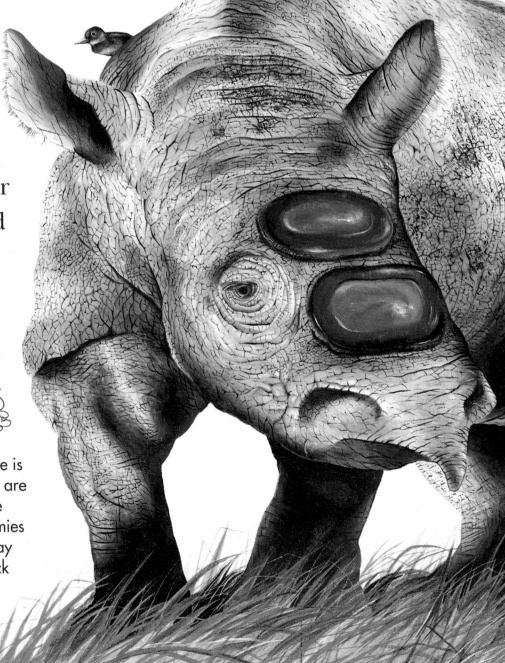

Rhinos live on the grasslands of Africa and Asia. It is against the law to hunt them, but some people still do. This is because they can get a lot of money for a rhino's horn. In some countries the horn is thought to be magical. It is carved into dagger handles or ground up for medicines.

● In some African nature reserves the rangers catch the rhinos and cut off their horns. It doesn't hurt the rhinos, and hopefully it will stop the poachers from killing them.

● The African pancake tortoise is endangered because so many are caught and sold as pets. In the wild it gets away from its enemies by hiding between rocks. It may fool other animals, but this trick doesn't work against the pet hunters.

Where can you shoot elephants?

Elephants are endangered because so many are killed for their ivory tusks. In most places it is against the law to shoot them – except with a camera. The money the tourists pay to see the elephants can be spent on protecting these animals from the poachers.

● Like many grassland animals, the great bustard is becoming endangered as its home is turned into farmland. Cattle trample on the nests and escaping birds often fly into overhead cables.

Which 'extinct' animal returned to the wild?

Père David's deer was once extinct in the wild. The only ones left lived in zoos and parks. Luckily they were bred so successfully that now they are being returned to their grassland homes in north China.

Why do tigers need corridors?

In India, many tigers live in reserves and national parks, where they are safe from hunters. The problem is that one park is often cut off from another. A 'corridor' is a strip of forest linking two parks. Tigers can travel along it to find food or mates.

How did the possum cross the road?

The rare mountain pygmy possum of Australia uses a subway. After a road was built through its reserve, the males kept getting run over when they went to visit the females. The subway was built and now they can cross the road safely.

- The Galápagos Islands in the Pacific Ocean are the home to plants and animals not found anywhere else in the world. The islands have been turned into a huge national park so all the wildlife is protected.

Why are gorillas not to be sniffed at?

Mountain gorillas live in reserves high up in the Virunga Mountains in Africa. People can visit them, but the gorillas are not used to common human illnesses. They can die of flu. To protect the gorillas, visitors have to show they're fit and healthy.

- There are probably fewer than 4,000 tigers left in India. They are protected by law, but poachers still kill them because their claws and bones can be sold to make medicines and the fur sells for lots of money too.

Why are polar bears still at risk?

Polar bears used to be hunted for their fur. That's stopped now and the biggest threat to them is the planet overheating due to pollution in the air. If the Arctic ice melts, the bears won't be able to roam freely in search of food.

Why do seals get their fur dyed?

In some areas of the Canadian Arctic, the pups of ringed seals are hunted for their pure white fur. People trying to protect the seals sometimes spray them with coloured dye. It doesn't hurt the baby seals, but it makes their fur useless to the hunters.

• In some areas, polar bears go into towns to scavenge for food. Hungry bears can be a danger to people. Some have to be shot, but most are just taken somewhere safer.

• People nearly hunted the musk ox to extinction until they realised they'd make more money from its thick, soft fur than its meat. They stopped killing the ox and now shear it like a sheep instead.

Which endangered whale has a unicorn's horn?

The narwhal is a kind of whale which lives in the Arctic seas. The males are hunted for their spiralled tusk which looks just like a unicorn's horn. If too many narwhals are taken, they may one day become extinct.

• Antarctica hasn't suffered as much from the harmful things that humans have done as other parts of the world. It is the last wilderness and many think it should stay that way.

KEEP OUT OF ANTARCTICA!

GO AWAY!

When do animals like going to the zoo?

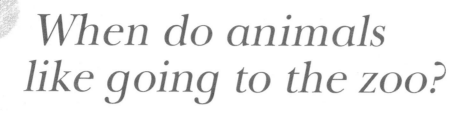

In the past, zoos kept animals just for people to look at. To some people, the animals looked cramped and lonely. Today, many zoos are working hard to breed endangered animals, such as tamarins, and hopefully return them to the wild. If animals could talk, they might say they preferred this kind of zoo.

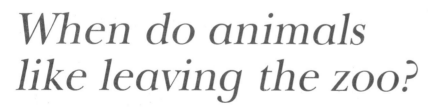

When do animals like leaving the zoo?

The last wild Arabian oryx was shot in 1972. Luckily, a few were rescued in time and were kept in zoos. They bred well and now a herd of over 100 roams the deserts of Oman once more.

• Sixty-five years ago, the golden hamster was nearly extinct. Then one female and her 12 young were caught and allowed to breed in safety. Soon there were millions of them!

Which endangered animal is brought up in a bucket?

Baby Kemp's ridley turtles are being raised in special hatcheries in the United States and Mexico. In their buckets, they are safe from seabirds and other hunters. When they are big enough to fend for themselves they are put into the ocean.

• Everyone thought the bridled nailtail wallaby, or flashjack, was extinct. Then a colony was discovered in 1973 near Dingo in eastern Australia. The area where they live is now protected.

Index

A

African elephant 6, 15
African grey parrot 40
African pancake tortoise 70
albatross 36
alligator 8
amphibian 8, 10, 21, 42
anaconda 45

anemone 25
angelfish 32
anhinga 22
ant 22
anteater 22
ape 9
Arabian camel 17
armadillo 47
aye-aye 21, 23

B

balance 19
bat 14, 21, 38, 63
bear 22, 65, 74, 75
bedbug 51
bee 22, 63

beetle 11, 52, 56, 57
bird 10, 22, 34–41, 59, 67, 71
birth 66

blue whale 6, 7, 60
body armour 25, 26
body temperature 43, 46
bombardier beetle 56
bone 11, 35
breathing 26, 60
bug 51
burrowing owl 67
butterfly 6, 37, 50, 52, 54, 55

C

camel 16,17
camouflage 12, 13, 31, 66
cat 34
caterpillar 54
cattle 71
centipede 11, 51
chameleon 13, 48
cheetah 18
chimpanzee 8, 58, 65
clam 32
clownfish 32, 33
cockroach 52
colour 13, 32, 54
communication 16, 60
coral 33
coral reef 32, 33
cougar 66
crab 9–11, 25, 29, 50
crocodile 8, 42, 44, 46
cub 64
Cuban bee hummingbird 37
cuckoo 59

D

damselfly 50
deer 66, 71
defence 11, 24, 25, 30, 31, 56, 66, 67, 70
dinosaur 7, 45, 53, 68

dolphin 26
down 40
dragonfly 50, 53, 61
duck-billed platypus 38
duckling 65

E

egg laying 38, 42, 53, 55, 57, 59
eider duck 37
elephant 6, 15, 16, 28, 62, 68, 71
endangered species 21, 69–77
exoskeleton 11
extinction 68, 71, 75–77
eyes 14, 15, 49

F

fairy fly 53
family group 62–63
fawn 66
feathers 38–41
fish 10, 22, 28, 30–32, 65
flamingo 13, 41
flea 18
flying 27, 34, 35, 40, 52, 55, 56
flying fox 21
food 16–23, 30, 41, 51, 54, 57, 59, 61, 65, 74, 75
food store 16, 17
frog 8, 21, 42
fur 13, 40, 74